YETI FOR BED

WRITTEN BY
WADE AND AMBER OLSEN

ILLUSTRATED BY
GIDEON BURNETT

THE DINNER DONE, THE SUN WAS SLIDING,
AND STARS BEGAN TO PEEK FROM HIDING.

SNOW BALLS WERE STACKED, THE FREEZER FILLED,
THE DISHES WASHED, THE LANTERNS CHILLED,
AND IN THE FROSTY MOONLIT NIGHT,

LITTLE YETI SQUEAKED,

"ALRIGHT."

DAD BLEW A KISS TO MOM,
THEN WENT WITH LITTLE YETI.
LITTLE FUZZY FOOTSTEPS RAN
TO GET THE BUBBLES READY.

LITTLE YETI SOAKED AND PLAYED,
HE WASHED HIS SHOULDERS TWICE.
HIS ELBOWS AND HIS CLAWS WERE SCRUBBED
UNTIL THEY SPARKLED NICE.

"COME HERE, YOU LITTLE STINKER!"

MOMMA NUZZLED IN WITH CARE,
THEN RUBBED HER PURPLE WOVEN TOWEL
ALL OVER YETI'S HAIR.

THE FUR WAS CLEAN AND CURLY,
FLOOFED FROM TOE TO SHOULDER.
INTO THE MIRROR YETI SQUEALED,

"I GREW!
I THINK
I'M OLDER!"

THEN TAKING TURNS THEY SMOOTHED THE KNOTS AND BRUSHED OUT YETI'S HAIR.

THEN PAPA SNARLED AND YETI CLAWED,
TO PRACTICE TERRORIZING.

is THERE TiME FOR BEDTiME SONGS?
BiG PAPA LOVES TO SiNG,

MOMMA SMOOTHED THE SHEETS
AND PILLOWS FOR THE LITTLE YETI,
THEN GLANCED INTO HER CHILD'S EYES AND SAID,

"YOU SURE LOOK READY!"

IT'S TIME TO READ A BEDTIME STORY
    FILLED WITH FUN ADVENTURE
WITH UNICORNS, AND MOOSE AND BEAR
    THEY REALLY ARE A TREASURE.

"GOOD NiGHT MOM AND PAPPA!"
SAYS LiTTLE YETi, YAWNiNG.
"GOOD NiGHT OUR LiTTLE PRECiOUS
ONE, WE'LL SEE YOU iN THE MORNiNG!"

YETi FACTS*

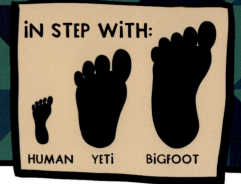

GENERAL FACTS:
YETi ARE HUMONGOUS! THEY ARE SOMETiMES CALLED AN "ABOMiNABLE SNOWMAN" WHiCH iS NOT VERY NiCE. THEY PREFER TO BE CALLED YETi. THEY ARE BiPEDAL WHiCH MEANS THAT THEY STAND ON THEiR HiND LEGS LiKE A HUMAN OR AN APE. THEiR COUSiNS ARE THE BiGFOOT, AND THOUGH THE YETi ARE BETTER MOUNTAiN CLiMBERS, A BiGFOOT OBViOUSLY HAS BiGGER FEET (iT'S PART OF THEiR NAME ATER ALL!)

HABiTAT:
YETi LOVE iCY WiND, BLiZZARDS AND ANYTHiNG COLD. THEY USUALLY LiVE ON GLACiERS OR ON HiGH MOUNTAiNS COVERED iN SNOW. THEY MOSTLY LiVE NEAR THE HiMiLAYAN MOUNTAiNS WHiCH iS WHERE MT. EVEREST iS- THE TALLEST MOUNTAiN iN THE WORLD. THEY LOVE TO LiVE iN COZY CAVES, CABiNS AND EVEN THE OCCASiONAL iGLOO.

SiZE:
ADULT YETi TOWER ABOVE HUMANS, STANDiNG BETWEEN NiNE TO ELEVEN FEET TALL! EVEN YOUNG YETi ARE SUPER TALL STANDiNG AROUND FiVE FEET TALL BY THE TiME THEY ARE SiX YEARS OLD.

*THESE FACTS ARE A HUNDRED PERCENT TRUE iN ANY WORLD iN WHiCH YETi EXiST, WHiCH, UNFORTUNATELY DOES NOT iNCLUDE THiS ONE (DARN!)

HOW BiG ARE YOU?

11 ft

6 ft

Adult Yeti   Adult Human   Yeti age 3   Human age 6

WHERE iN THE WORLD iS MOUNT EVEREST?